Training Wheels Alphabet Book

A Unique, Space-Age Approach
to Learning to Read and Write

Text and Illustrations

by

Wendell H. Hall

WestBow
PRESS
A DIVISION OF THOMAS NELSON

Cover and interior art by Wendell Hall.

WestBow Press books may be ordered through booksellers or by contacting:

WestBow Press
A Division of Thomas Nelson
1663 Liberty Drive
Bloomington, IN 47403
www.westbowpress.com
1 (866) 928-1240

ISBN: 978-1-4908-1385-1 (sc)
ISBN: 978-1-4908-1386-8 (e)

Library of Congress Control Number: 2013919253

Printed in the United States of America.

WestBow Press rev. date: 1/7/2014

Dedicated with admiration and love to granddaughter Charlotte Brooks Parker,

the first teacher to use this book (preliminary version) in her classes.

Introduction

English is a very difficult language to learn to read and write. The root of the problem is that our alphabet has only 26 letters and at least half that many more are required in order to represent all of our language's phonemes or contrasting sets of sounds. This has given rise to all kinds of strange combinations of vowels and consonants, including silent letters and other unnecessary complications and confusions. A detailed study by Godfrey Dewey* demonstrates that instead of an ideal one to one grapheme-phoneme relationship of 40-40, we have 561 for 40.

A teacher or tutor cannot always be standing by to guide learners through the complexities of a spelling that has been thoroughly mixed up and messed up for centuries, nor is it feasible to expect children to memorize and apply rules that baffle, confuse, and turn off adults. Moreover, there are aggravating exceptions to every rule that can trip up the best of spellers. A totally wierd predicament, right? Or is that *weird?* So much for "I before E except after C."

No one could climb on a bike put together from 26 parts functioning in 561 unpredictable ways and learn to ride it smoothly and effortlessly within a year or even ten years. Analogously, is it any wonder that approximately 30% of our high school graduates lack proficiency in reading and that an estimated 40,000,000 Americans above the age of 15 are functional illiterates, unable to read and fill out relatively simple job applications? Shouldn't it mortify us to the very core to know that so-called third-world countries like Bolivia and Cuba are leaving us behind in terms of literacy, thanks mainly to the fact that Spanish has a nearly perfect spelling system? Can anyone doubt therefore that we urgently need to reform our English ~~system~~?

So what do we do to help a little child learn to ride even a perfect bicycle? The answer is simple: We get some training wheels for them and then stay right at their side, lending instant support, encouragement and praise, steadying them as necessary, keeping them from falling or getting discouraged and doing our utmost to help them experience the thrill of going it alone as speedily and effectively as possible. As teachers, parents, tutors and other helpers, we fully share in their sense of achievement—along with a touch of pride—and make our feelings unambiguously known to them.

The Training Wheels Alphabet Book takes the embarrassing, scandalous mess of our centuries-old English spelling and makes it glide along as though it had only 26 simple, uncomplicated parts—one function per part. The only exceptions allowed are the digraphs *ck, ff, ll, nn, tt* and *zz.* Our traditional English spelling is so irregular that only by accepting a few relatively minor aberrations like this is it possible to put together more than a hundred or so coherent, only slightly irregularly-spelled words and sentences. The remaining bizarre, absurdly excessive letter-sound correspondences (561 minus 26) are introduced with **The *Look, Mom, No Hands!* Alphabet Book** and **Easy Speedy Readers®**.

---

*English Spelling: Roadblock to Reading. Teachers College Press. Teachers College, Columbia University. New York. 1971.

i

The 26 letter-sound correspondences employed in **The Training Wheels Alphabet Book** are the most frequent ones. For example, the letter A stands for its sound in *at* rather than *ate, above, or always*; E represents that of *met*, not *meet, meat* or *deceit*; I is as in *lit* not *light* or *kilo;* O, *tot* not *tote, toot, took* or *love;* U, *cut* not *cute* or *dude*. The sound of *S* is always as in *hiss*, never *his, sugar, pleasure,* etc. The spellings *psychology, schism, sword* and such, naturally, are absent. Exceptions: *ax, fox,* etc., which really should have *ks,* but *x* remains to save a keystroke and for math. Any task as complex as learning to read, spell and write English should start with the known, simple and easy and lead only gradually to the unfamiliar, complex and difficult. To assure mastery, each step should be repeated several times and reviewed periodically. Memory aids should be employed to the fullest extent. Words and letters should be tied phonetically, denotatively, grammatically and visually by means of matching sounds, synonyms, antonyms, subjects-verbs, verbs-objects, adjectives-nouns, etc. plus numerous non-complex graphic representations.

An ancient mnemonic device (aid to memory) has been resurrected as a key element of instruction. Though the history of writing has been the object of much research, the origin of the alphabet remains somewhat obscure. Some experts believe that acrophony* entered into its development. This is somewhat analogous (in reverse) to vocally converting single letters to single words for clarification against a background of static or noise. For example, *Infantry Company A* becomes *Able* or *Alpha* and *Company B* is *Baker* or *Bravo*.

In acrophony, single sounds are represented in the opposite way. Borrowing Semitic symbols that stood for the initial sounds of the words *ox, house, camel,* etc., the Greeks developed the letters from which (through Latin) our modern ABCs are basically derived. Semitic *alef* (ox) and *beth* (house) became Greek *alpha* and *beta,* from which the word *alphabet* was coined. In some examples of ancient writing, an apparent evolution from picture to phonetic symbol is present. Although not all authorities agree that this happened with *alef,* it takes little imagination to picture the head of an ox, with ears and horns, in the symbol ⋉

This was altered by the Greeks and Romans until it became A. The use of memory aids was highly developed in ancient times and it has been theorized that ⋉ , for example, might have been consciously designed to suggest an *aleph's* head as a cue to phonetic [a]. In modern times this idea has been used very successfully by the great promoter of literacy Charles L. Laubach for rapidly teaching different alphabets to millions of learners around the world. (Everyone should read his fascinating, stimulating book *The Silent Billion*. With "billion" he makes reference to all those around the world who have little voice in anything at all because they are unable to read and write**.) The Training Wheels Alphabet Book** makes further, modified use of a system which evidently had its origin in the remote past.

To reiterate a point already made above, along with good training wheels, nothing is more important than a loving mother or father, older brother or sister, teacher, tutor or

---

*The ingenious idea to let graphic depictions of selected things stand not for the items themselves but for the initial sounds. So a pictograph for "snake" could eventually come to indicate only the first sound, S.

friend to run alongside lending words of encouragement and appreciation, giving pats on the back, helping to get the bike over rough spots, difficult turns and slippery turf. Learning to ride a bike is one of the greatest thrills of childhood, not far behind taking our first step. In both instances, without the admiring applause of people who care, the achievement lacks the luster it ought to have. In the future, when these materials are computerized, they will be programmed for interaction with others to assure that this element is not lacking. Yes, the computer can "morph" a snake right into an S, produce speech, the hissing of a snake or other sounds indicative of phonetic values and provide all kinds of ways to applaud correct answers and calculate and display scores. But if learners are deprived of appreciative, attentive, caring support and confirmation directly from other humans, give me paper over electronics anytime.

To facilitate dialog and interaction and to clarify what a given picture is intended to represent, inasmuch as graphic ambiguity is difficult to eliminate, brief notes are given at the bottom of each page. They are intended only to stimulate adlibbing superior to mine on the part of teachers and tutors. Examples:

Page 1. Point to the belt. "What does this look like? A belt... It has a funny shape, like a belt that had to fit inside a suitcase or something. What's the first sound of *belt*? That's right. Buh..." (Pronounce it *buh,* not *bee,* with just a slight, unstressed vowel—the most common vowel in English, for which we have no letter and which can be spelled many different ways, for example as *e* in *open* or the second *o* of *option.* Linguists refer to it as *schwa* and give it this symbol: ə. /ti/ in the above example has the value of sh, or ʃ in the International Phonetic Alphabet.) "Try that again. Bə... bə... bə... Belt."

Learners should be taught the traditional name of each letter, but these are not very helpful in terms of sounding out words, so the consonants are pronounced with an accompanying schwa and a, e, i, o, u are rendered as indicated above; i.e., as in *at, met, it, cot, cut.*

"Now look at this one. Can you tell what it is? Let me give you a hint. If I say it's something used to cook with, you'll know right off that it's a... Right! A pan. Or maybe it's a pot. I think a pan has a long handle like this and a pot has a little handle on each side, or something like that. Anyway, what's the first sound of pan or pot? Pə... Pot. Pə... pə... Pan. That's an easy one, isn't it? A pan, hanging from a hook.

"The last one here is a little harder. It looks like someone might have used it to wrap a pretty package. Do you think it's a piece of... Ribbon! You guess right every time! It's shaped like maybe it went around a present once and there are two loose ends where it was tied. Can you say ribbon again? Very good! Ribbon." (If a child has difficulty with this sound and says "wibbon," that's quite O.K. for now.) "What's the first sound of ribbon? Rə... rə... rə... ribbon. That's great! I can see I won't have to tie a ribbon around your finger for you to remember that.

"Now look at this (the P). Does it remind you of a belt, a pan, or a ribbon? A pan... It looks a little bit like a pan, hanging from a peg. What's the first sound of pan again? Pə...

iii

Take a good look at this letter. It's part of what we call the alphabet or the ABCs. It stands for pə. When you are reading and see this letter, called P (pea), you'll know that almost always it's for pə. Very soon we'll put pə together with other sounds so that they'll say something. Maybe top or pop or spot.

"Take a good look at these pictures. I'm sure you know what each thing is, but in order to learn alphabet sounds we're going to choose some names over others. We could call this one a hat or a cap, but we're going to say cap. Can you guess why? Is there a pə sound in hat? No. But... Yes, you're absolutely right. There is in cap.

"How about these other ones? Do you know what this thing is that looks sort of like a cup with a long handle? I'll give you a clue. It's a də.... A dip.... A dipper! Yes, and this helps you to remember the sound of P, which most of the time is pə." (There's no need, obviously, to go into spellings like *photo* now—nor of *pneumatic*, *psyche*, etc. until much later.)

Page 2. "What's this? A leg. Can you say Lə? lə... lə... lə... as in *leg*. Beautiful! Can you think of anything else that starts with lə? *Look?* Oh, that's a good one. How about this?" (Point to your lip.) "Right! Lip. Lə.. lə... lə... Lip."

Show the learner(s) a ruler. "This next one (point to representation of *inch*) is part of a ruler. A ruler is to measure things with. Let's measure your hand. Why it's almost four inches long! See? One, two, three, and almost four. Each of these is an inch. And this is a drawing of an inch. Let's see if you can say *inch*. Iii... iii... iii... Inch.

"Does this one look like a nail or a tack? Right on! A tack usually isn't as long as a nail and it has a large head—most of the time flat. O.K. You know how we do this. Go right ahead. Tə... Right you are! The first sound of *tack* is tə.

"All right, O.K.! Does *eye* have a tə in it? Does *tie*?" Etc.

Page 3. "See this? It's salty and sometimes these are stuffed with red pimento. It's an... Olive! *Ah...liv.* The first sound is... *ah...* Say it again.
"I know you don't need any help with this one. Sure! An umbrella. The first sound of *olive* is *ah* and the first sound of *umbrella* is... Right! *Uh... uh... umbrella.*

"Remember that picture from the other page, the thing with a long handle? This shows only the bottom part of it. It was a də... A dipper! You're right, as usual. Take a good look at the shape of it. This will help us to learn the sound of another new letter that we'll come to before very long.

"Here we go again. Which of the three things looks most like the letter in the last frame? This one. The olive! Right again. We call this letter O (oh) and sometimes it has this sound but most often it's like the first sound of *olive*." (In General American English or GA, the name given to the variety of English most widely spoken in the United States, no significant distinction is made between the *a* of *father* and the *o* of *cot*. In geographical regions and instances where these contrast, have learners pronounce the words as they always do.)

"All right. Let's see. For this lesson, do you think this animal is called a cow, a bull or an ox? Right you are, and this other one could be a dog or a f.... A fox! Looks like someone tried to draw a fox. Hmmm. Maybe in preparation for *x* later on."

(Review the first three letters in the box at the bottom.)

"Does this last one remind you of anything? Something that wriggles or snakes its way along on the ground and makes a hissing sound? Ssss. The first sound of its name is also *sssss*. A snake, of course! Well, you've learned this letter already, before we even get to its page. It's probably the easiest one to learn and remember."

Page 4. "Now the real fun begins, because we're going to start to put all this together. Look at these three drawings and the letters they help us to remember. They can go together to make words. Look at this one with the number 1 by it. What is the sound of the first letter? Tə! Now the second and the third. Tə O [as in hot] Pə. Now say the sounds faster, without separating them. TOP! All right! Hurrah! I'm going to give you a high [5]! Wonderful! Congratulations! You have just learned one of the most important things you'll ever learn: The basic key to reading English and all other languages that use an alphabet for reading and writing. The whole world of books and magazines, the worlds of work, of fun… of learning about all there is to learn about will soon be open to you!

"O.K., you've now got a foot in the door to so many things! Now all you have to do is point to the picture that goes with TOP." (As mentioned in the footnotes on several pages, learners may practice the numbers and the letters in giving their answers. If these are written lightly and then erased, it will be easy for other learners to reuse the same materials or for the same ones to reuse them for review.)

These ideas for interaction should be sufficient to get you started. In addition to the illustrations in the book, try to use objects, actions, pantomime, chalkboards, overhead projectors, etc. as much as possible. Also, have learners cut out pictures from magazines for illustrating certain words, brief phrases and sentences. At a more advanced level they thoroughly enjoy putting together color pencil or crayon illustrated story books. I have found that the use of labelers to imprint block letters on brightly colored plastic tape is an excellent device to help learners get started with writing—and they love it. They can then stick appropriate labels on pictures, objects and… on Grandpa, I have discovered. Some models of labelers fit smaller hands.

Off to a great start with the help of **Training Wheels**, learners figuratively will soon be racing confidently and smoothly around as well as excitedly doing wheelie boppers. To truly reach that stage, however, they need to complete **The *Look, Mom, No Hands! Alphabet Book***. Then a series of Easy Speedy Readers® commencing with **Poor Little Sick Boy** will propel them rapidly onward toward full achievement of this goal.

BASIC LETTER SHAPES AND SOUNDS

AX	GLOVE	LEG	QUINCE	VEST
BELT	HINGE	MOUNTAINS	RIBBON	WINGS
COLLAR	INCH	NOODLE	SNAKE	X-OUT
DIPPER	JAR	OLIVE	TACK	YOKE
END TABLE	KINDLING	PAN	UMBRELLA	ZIGZAG
FLAG	SHIN	CHIN	QUINCE	

P T O STOP

1. TOP

2. POT

3. POP

O P T S

1. POTS

2. TOPS

3. SPOT

6

7

I S T P

1 PIT

2 TIP

3 SIP

8

1 POT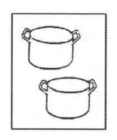

2 PIT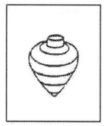

3 TIP

4 TOP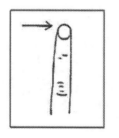

5 POP

6 SPOT

7 SIP

8 SIS

9 POTS

10 SPOTS

11 TOPS

12 TOSS

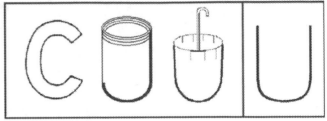

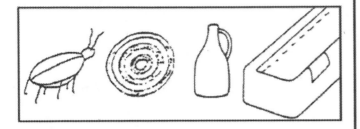

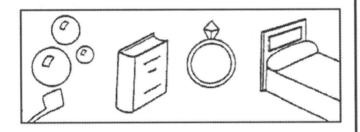

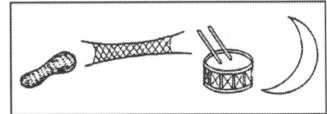

1 BIB

1 BUS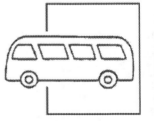

2 BIT

2 TUB

3 SOB

3 PUP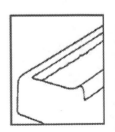

10

↕↔	B	T	U	S	I	P	O
S							
I							
O							
P							
B							
T							
U							

1 POP IT!
2 TOP IT!
3 TIP IT!

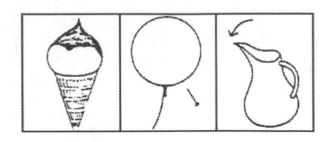

1 SIT IT UP!
2 SOP IT UP!
3 SIP IT UP!

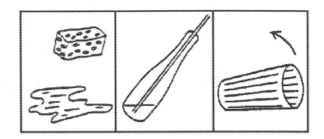

1 SPOT IT!
2 PUTT IT!
3 STOP IT!

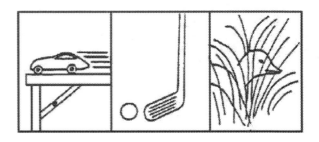

1 BUS IT!
2 SIP IT!
3 PIT IT!

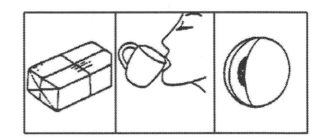

1 SPOT IT UP!
2 STOP IT UP!
3 TIP IT UP!

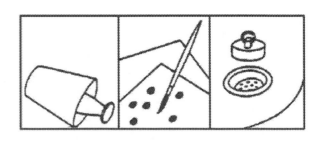

1 BOSS IT!
2 TOSS IT!
3 BUTT IT!

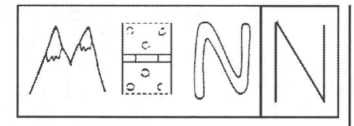 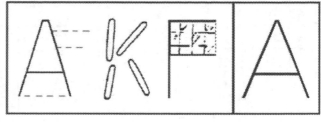

1 NUT

1 ANT

2 PIN

2 PAN

3 SUN

3 BAT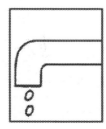

4 NUN

4 TAP

5 BUN

5 NAP

13

1 TOT

2 PAT

3 SUB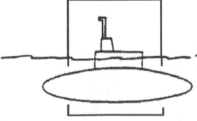

4 BIN

5 SAP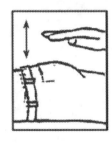

6 BASS

7 SNAP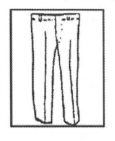

8 SNIP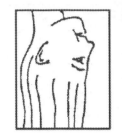

9 PANTS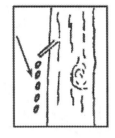

10 SPAT

11 STUB

12 STUNT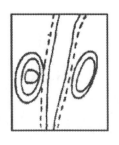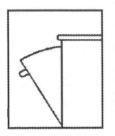

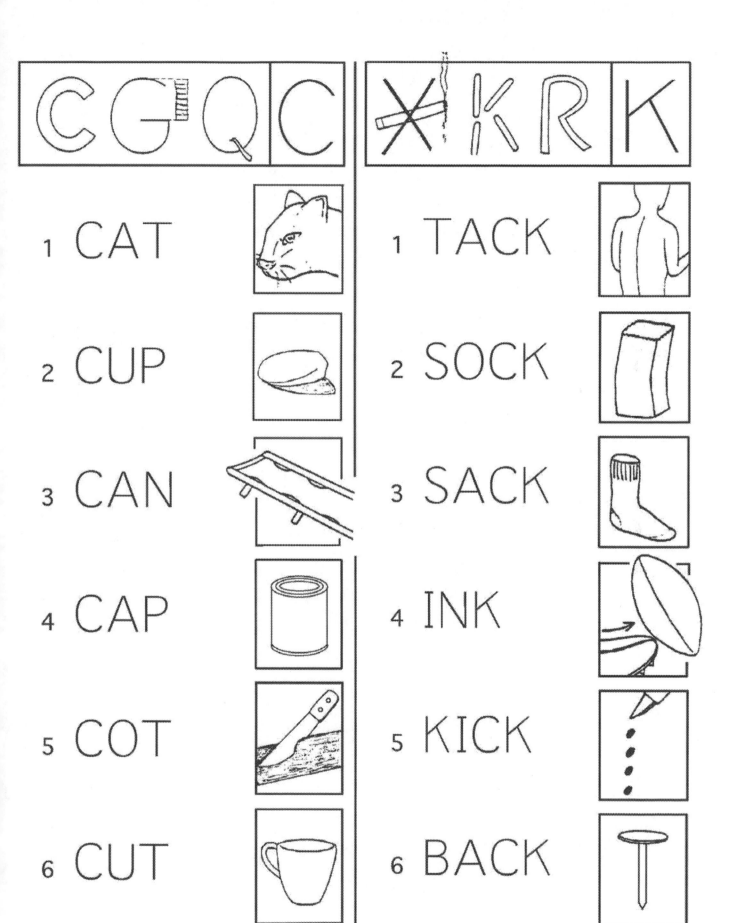

C G Q | C

1 CAT
2 CUP
3 CAN
4 CAP
5 COT
6 CUT

K R | K

1 TACK
2 SOCK
3 SACK
4 INK
5 KICK
6 BACK

15

1 COB

2 CAB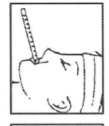

3 PICK

4 PACK

5 SICK

6 SINK

7 TANK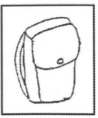

8 KISS

9 BUNK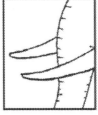

10 SKUNK

11 STICK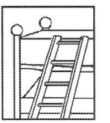

12 TUSKS

13 PICNIC

14 NAPKIN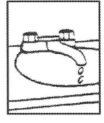

16

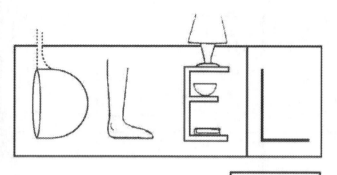 

1 LIP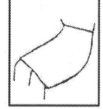

2 LAP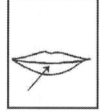

3 PILL

4 LIST

5 SLIP

6 BULB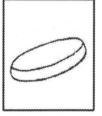

7 BAG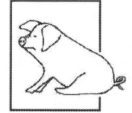

8 BUG

9 GUN

10 PIG

11 LOG

12 PLUG

17

	A	B	C	G	K	L	N
G							
N							
L							
B							
C							
K							
A							

18

1 PAN		SACK
2 PANTS		TOP
3 COT		SUCK
4 BAG		TOSS
5 CAP		CUT
6 ANT		SPANK
7 SNIP		SLACKS
8 TILT		BUG
9 PASS		TIP
10 SLOP		POT
11 SPAT		SPILL
12 SIP		BUNK

19

1 CLAP!
2 SLAP IT!
3 SUCK ON IT!

1 PAT IT!
2 KISS IT!
3 SPANK IT!

1 BAT IT!
2 PASS IT!
3 SPIN IT!

1 PIN IT ON!
2 TUCK IT IN!
3 LOCK IT UP!

1 SIT UP IN IT!
2 PULL IN ON IT!
3 STAND UP AT IT!

1 SINK IN IT!
2 MUST NOT SLIP ON IT!
3 SLIP IT ON!

1 TUG ON IT!
2 STOP AT IT!
3 SKIP UP IT!

1 SIT STILL UNTIL IT STOPS!
2 PULL TILL IT UNLOCKS!
3 LICK IT UNTIL IT STICKS!

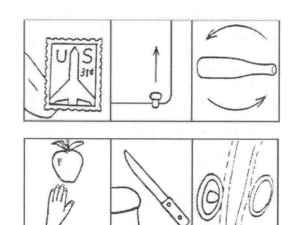

1 ANN CAN CUT IT.
2 BOB CAN'T PICK IT
3 NAN CAN'T SNAP IT.

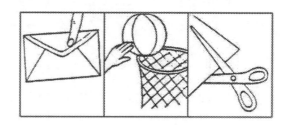

1 STICK IT TILL IT'S STUCK!
2 TIP IT UP UNTIL IT'S IN!
3 SNIP IT TILL IT'S CUT!

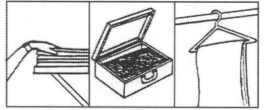

1 SCOTT PACKS BLACK PANTS.
2 JILL PICKS PINK SLACKS.
3 SIS STACKS SILK SLIPS.

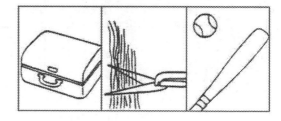

1 CAN GUS CLIP IT?
2 CAN SAL UNPACK IT?
3 CAN AL BUNT IT?

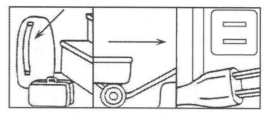

1 PLUG IT BACK IN!
2 LUG IT UP LAST!
3 TUG IT ON PAST!

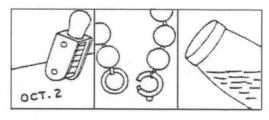

1 GIB CAN STAMP IT.
2 PAT CAN'T SPILL IT.
3 BAB CAN CLASP IT.

 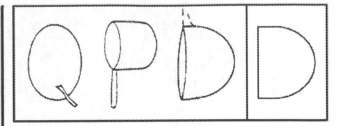

1	EGG		1	DOLL	
2	LEG	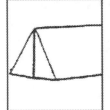	2	BED	
3	NECK	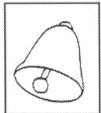	3	DOG	
4	BELL	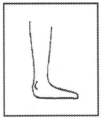	4	DOT	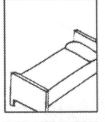
5	PEN	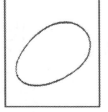	5	LID	
6	TENT		6	DESK	

22

1	CLOCKS		BEND
2	SKUNKS		KISS
3	BATS		CLOG
4	SINKS		STINK
5	LIPS		TICK
6	BACKS		SPIN
7	TOPS		BUNT

1	SIT ON		LIPS
2	SPIN		PETS
3	KILL		SINKS
4	PAT		PESTS
5	PLUS		TOPS
6	LICK		POP
7	SIP		LAPS

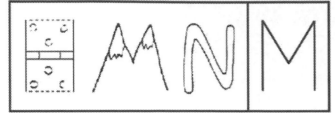 

1 MILK

2 GUM

3 MOP

4 MASK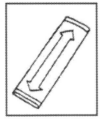

5 PLUM

6 LAMP

1 RAT

2 ROCK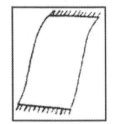

3 DRUM

4 DRESS

5 RUG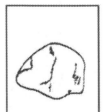

6 GRASS

1 DOG    CRIB

2 CAT      CUP

3 MAT    KITTEN

4 MUG      PUP

5 BED    END

6 TIP   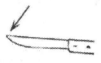   RUG

---

1 CRACK   GRASS

2 DIM    MUD

3 DRINK   LAMPS

4 MEND   NUTS

5 PLANT 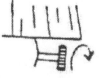   SOCKS

6 GET STUCK IN    MILK

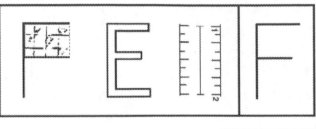 F 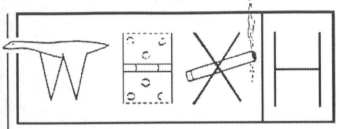 H

1 FLAG

1 HAM

2 CUFF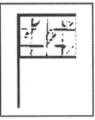

2 HAND

3 FROG

3 HAT

4 FAN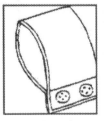

4 HEN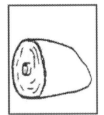

5 FIST

5 HILL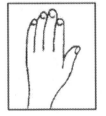

6 FIG

6 HUT

↕ ↔	D	E	F	F	H	M	N	R
E								
N								
H								
M								
R								
D								
F								

1 SMELL

2 SPILL

3 FILL

4 HUG

5 CROSS

6 PRESS

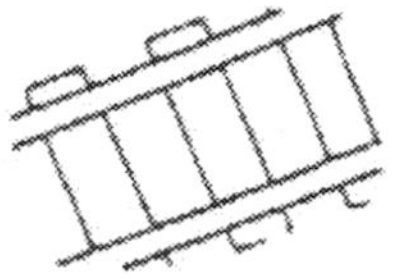

CUPS

TRACKS

SLACKS

MILK

HOT DOG

MOM

1 CAP

2 HOG

3 FIST

4 FROCK

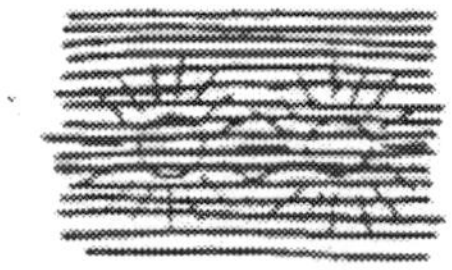

5 LUMP

6 MIST

FOG

HAT

PIG

BUMP

HAND

DRESS

1 DAD DROPS US OFF.
2 PAM ASKS US IN.
3 MOM PICKS US UP.

1 KIT AND PAT MUST HELP MOM.
2 KIT DUSTS AND PAT MOPS.
3 KIT'S GLAD BUT PAT'S MAD.

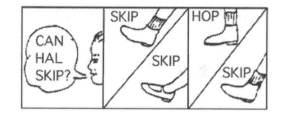

1 IF HAL CAN SKIP, TESS CAN.
2 DAN ASKS IF HAL CAN SKIP.
3 HAL CAN HOP AND SKIP.

1 MOM HELPS RON GET IN BED.
2 RON MUST NOT ROMP.
3 RON MUST REST.

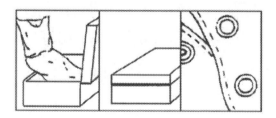

1 DOT CAN'T DRESS TILL MOM UNPACKS.
2 MOM UNPACKS DOT'S BEST DRESS.
3 MOM HELPS DOT SNAP IT UP IN BACK.

1 TIM CAN'T UNDRESS HIMSELF BUT DON CAN.
2 DON CAN UNDRESS AND GET IN BED.
3 MOM AND DAD HUG HIM AND TUCK HIM IN.

1 MOM PACKS KIT'S PINK BAG.
2 KIT HELPS MOM STUFF IT FULL.
3 KIT LOCKS ITS BRASS CLASPS.

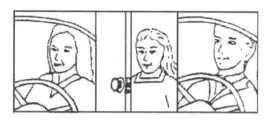

1 ERIC'S FAT CAT HUNTS RATS.
2 IT HUMPS ITS BACK.
3 IT LICKS ITS LIPS.

1 PAT'S KITTEN LAPS UP ITS MILK.
2 IT FLOPS ON ITS BACK.
3 IT SNIFFS AT CATNIP.

1 HANK'S TOMCAT HAD A CATNAP.
2 IT SLEPT ON ITS SOFT MAT.
3 IT FELT SNUG AND PLUMP.

1 GRANT'S HEN STEPS OFF ITS NEST.
2 IT CLUCKS AND PECKS.
3 IT LEFT AN EGG IN ITS NEST.

1 RICK'S DOG CAN'T BEND ITS STIFF LEG.
2 IT LIIMPS AND CAN NOT RUN.
3 IT CAN SIT UP AND BEG.

1 GET IT, SPOT! GET KENT'S STICK!
2 SPOT CAN RUN FAST.
3 SPOT CAN PICK UP KENT'S STICK.

1 GREG'S RABBIT FELT FULL AND
    CONTENT.
2 GREG FED IT SCRAPS AND GRASS.
3 IT HID IN ITS PEN TILL ANN LEFT.

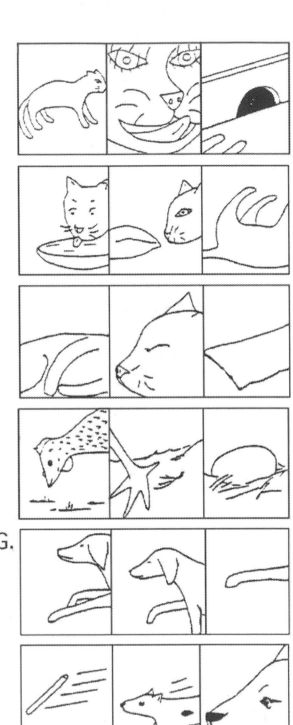

 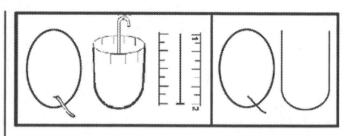

1 JUG		1 QUILT	
2 JAM		2 QUILL	
3 JET		3 QUACK	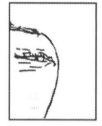
4 JUMP	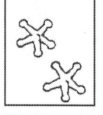	4 QUICK	
5 JUNK		5 SQUID	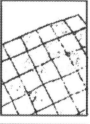
6 JACKS		6 SQUINT	

31

1	STICK		INSECT
2	DOT		STRAP
3	QUILT		STAFF
4	BELT		SPOT
5	STUMP		BLANKET
6	PEST		LOG

1	CLOG		SPLIT
2	CRACK		LIFT
3	JAB		GRASP
4	JACK		PLUG
5	JOG		HIT
6	GRIP		RUN

1 RIP, RIP. TOM RIPS UP STRIPS.

2 SNIP, SNIP. SIS SNIPS SCRAPS AND BITS.

3 LAP, LAP. SCOTT'S KITTEN LAPS UP ITS MILK.

4 SOB, SOB. JAN CAN ACT SAD AND SOB.

5 PAT, PAT. HANK'S HAND PATS SPOT'S BACK.

 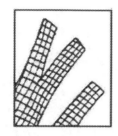 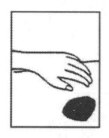  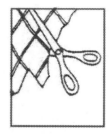

1 CLIP, CLIP. CLIFF CLIPS UNCUT GRASS.

2 NIP, NIP. NICK'S PUP NIPS AT NICK'S LEG.

3 FLIP, FLIP. FRED FLIPS AN ELASTIC AT MACK'S HAT.

4 LIMP, LIMP. ROCK'S DOG BROCK LIMPS AND CAN NOT RUN.

5 SLIP, SLIP. MEG SLIPS BUT GETS BACK UP.

  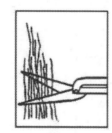  

1 NAP, NAP. FRAN'S PLASTIC DOLL SITS ON PAT'S LAP.

2 SLAM, SLAM. BRET HAD BETTER NOT SLAM IT.

3 RUN, RUN, PUFF, PUFF. RON RAN UPHILL AND MUST REST. ZZZZ, ZZZZ.

4 FLICK, FLICK. DICK'S LAMP FLICKS OFF AND ON.

5 TACK, TACK. DAD HELPS BESS TACK IT ON.

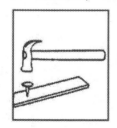 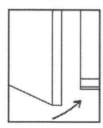   

 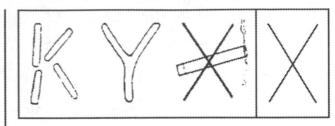

1 WIG 	1 BOX 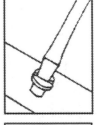
2 WEB 	2 AX 
3 WELL 	3 WAX 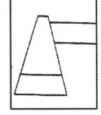
4 WAG 	4 FOX 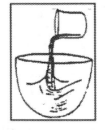
5 WINK 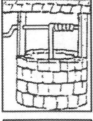	5 MIX 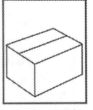
6 SWING 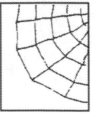	6 FIX 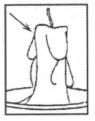

1 TRUCKS			STICK
2 TAPS			RIP
3 PANTS			HONK
4 JUNK			RUSTS
5 FROST	HONK HONK		MELTS
6 STAMPS			DRIP

---

1 WIN			MUD
2 WET		1	TRUNKS
3 MIX			FLATS
4 MOP UP			PLANTS
5 UNPACK			DRINKS
6 PUMP UP			CONTESTS

35

1 TIP, TIP. WILT TIPS IT UP AND IN.

2 PUFF, PUFF, FLAP, FLAP. PUFF, WIND, AND FLAP JACK'S FLAG.

3 MIX, MIX. MOM WILL MIX MILK AND HAM AND AN EGG.

4 WINK, WINK. DAD TRICKS NELL AND WINKS.

5 DRIP, DRIP. DROPS DRIP ON MAX AND GET HIM WET.

   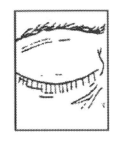 

1 QUACK, QUACK. DUCKS SWIM PAST US AND QUACK.

2 TICK TOCK. MILT'S CLOCK WENT TICK TOCK AND DIDN'T STOP.

3 NOD, NOD. SAND MAN AND AN ELF DROP SOFT SAND ON JAN.

4 DING DONG. WINT'S ELECTRIC BELL WENT DING DONG.

5 HOP, HOP, SKIP SKIP, JUMP, JUMP. GWEN CAN HOP, SKIP AND JUMP.

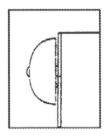    

1 BAM, BAM! CLINT'S SIXGUN WENT BAM, BAM, BAM, BAM, BAM, BAM!

2 RUB, RUB. MOM WILL RUB BRENT'S STIFF NECK.

3 FIX, FIX. DAD WILL FIX KENT'S CRIB.

4 MOP, MOP. ROXANN MUST HELP MOM MOP.

5 DUST, DUST, WAX, WAX. NEXT, ROXANN WILL DUST AND WAX.

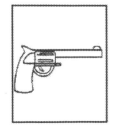 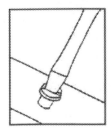 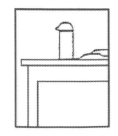 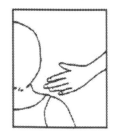 

1 FAT			UPSET
2 ILL			DAMP
3 SWIFT			CONTENT
4 GLAD			QUICK
5 WET			SICK
6 MAD			PLUMP

---

1 TOP			GLAD
2 FAT		NO PILLS OR MEDICINE	LIMP
3 ILL			BOTTOM
4 SAD			WELL
5 STIFF			OFF
6 ON			SLIM

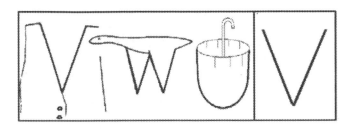

V

1 VEST

2 VAN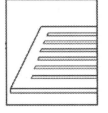

3 VAT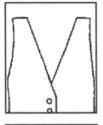

4 VENT

1 YELL

2 YAM

3 YAK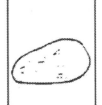

 **Z**

1 FEZ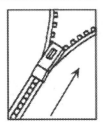

2 FIZZ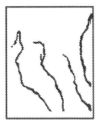

3 FUZZ

4 ZIP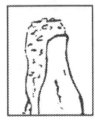

1 HOP

2 HUM

3 MEND

4 SNIFF

5 PLOP

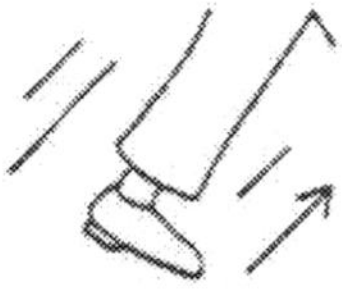

6 NOD

7 MOP

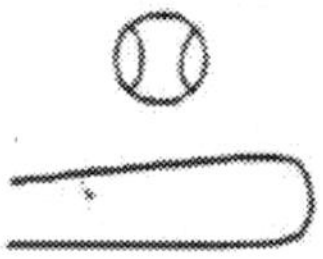

8 BEND

9 PRICK

10 DRINK

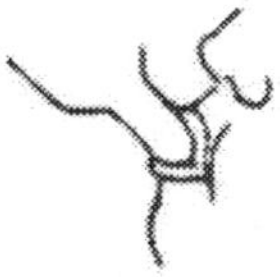

11 BAT

12 STUFF

FIX

SCRUB

NAP

PACK

BUNT

SMELL

FLOP

BUZZ

TWIST

STICK

SWIG

JUMP

	U	Q	V	W	X	Y	Z
W							
Z							
V							
J							
X							
Y							
Q							

1 POP! POP! WES AND ZEB POP SACKS.

2 KISS, KISS. LIZ AND VAL KISS MOM AND DAD.

3 YELL, YELL! DAD CAN TELL GRIFF'S YELL FROM CLINT'S.

4 FAN, FAN. IT'S HOT AND FRAN WILL FAN DAN.

5 FUSS, FUSS. SID WILL FUSS UNLESS MOM HELPS HIM.

  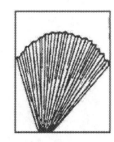  

1 LICK, LICK. SPOT WILL LICK RICK'S HAND.

2 GRIN, GRIN. AL CAN'T HELP BUT GRIN AT VIC'S TRICKS.

3 PAT, PAT. PATS ON HACK'S BACK HELP AND LIFT HIM UP, NOT SPATS AND SPANKS.

4 ZIP, ZIP. MOM ZIPS UP DOT'S DRESS IN BACK.

5 HUFF, HUFF, PUFF, PUFF! HUFF AND PUFF, BIG BAD WOLF!

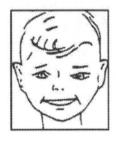    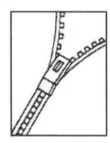

1 YUM, YUM, SMELL, SMELL! MEL CAN SMELL ZACK'S HOT CROSS BUN.

2 HONK, HONK, ZIP, ZIP! BUCK'S TRUCK WILL ZIP ON PAST US.

3 CRACK, CRACK. MOM WILL CRACK AN EGG AND FIX IT FOR GRIFF.

4 YUM, YUM, SMELL, SMELL! SMELL ROLF'S RED HOT HOT DOG!

5 BUZZ, BUZZ. BUZZ OFF, BLACK BUG, AND GET LOST!

    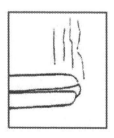

1 VAN		EXAM
2 TWIG		KICK
3 MAN	ADD: 2 / 5	SAND
4 TEST		TRUCK
5 DUST		DAD
6 PUNT		STEM

1 WINK		SKIN
2 CUT		PEN
3 QUEST		SLIT
4 QUILL	BIG POND / HILL / X	BLINK
5 PELT		BIT
6 HUNK		HUNT

1 JEFF CAN'T DRESS HIMSELF YET.
2 MOM MUST HELP HIM
3 JEFF'S STILL JUST SIX.

1 DOT'S DOLL ACTS SICK.
2 DOT PROPS IT UP IN BED.
3 IT MUST REST AND GET WELL.

1 JAN GOT POP.
2 REX DRANK MILK.
3 GWEN HAD AN EGGNOG.

1 WILL'S TRUCK WILL NOT RUN.
2 IT GOT HIT AND BENT IN BACK.
3 WILL MUST JACK IT UP AND FIX IT.

1 TRIX HAD TEN JACKS.
2 TRIX LEFT SEVEN IN WILL'S TRUCK.
3 WILL SENT BACK SIX.

1 JACK'S JACKET JUST FITS HIM.
2 JACK GOT IT LAST SEPTEMBER.
3 IT'S BLACK AND RED.

1 JILL ACTS CROSS AND SPATS PAT'S DOLL.
2 PAT GETS UPSET AND JILL STOPS.
3 PAT AND JILL TELL MOM IT'S JUST IN FUN.

1 TRUCKS DRIFT

2 JACKS  FIX

3 AN AX LIFT

4 BANKS  WILT

5 DUCKS  LEND

6 DRINKS  DRIFTS

7 SAND PUFFS

8 PICKS CUTS

9 BUMPS  DIG

10 PLANTS SWELL

11 RAFTS  QUACK

12 WIND  RUN

1 BLACK BUG, BLACK BUG,
SNUG IN ITS RUG,
IT'S SELDOM BAD
UNLESS IT'S MAD.

2 BLACK BUG, BLACK BUG,
SNUG IN ITS RUG
TRIPS ON ITS HAT
AND STOMPS IT FLAT.

3 BLACK BUG, BLACK BUG,
SNUG IN ITS RUG,
JUMPS UP AND HOPS
UNTIL IT FLOPS.

4 BLACK BUG, BLACK BUG,
SNUG IN ITS JUG,
IT IT GETS WET,
IT ACTS UPSET.

5 BLACK BUG, BLACK BUG,
SNUG ON ITS RUG,
IF IT'S NOT WELL,
ITS NECK WILL SWELL.

6 BLACK BUG, BLACK BUG,
SNUG IN ITS RUG,
IF IT GETS DAMP,
WILL YELL AND STAMP.

7 BLACK BUG, BLACK BUG,
SMUG IN ITS RUG.
! ! ! ! !
BUG OFF, BLACK BUG!

45

1 BENT    BULB

2 SWIFT    RAG

3 TIN 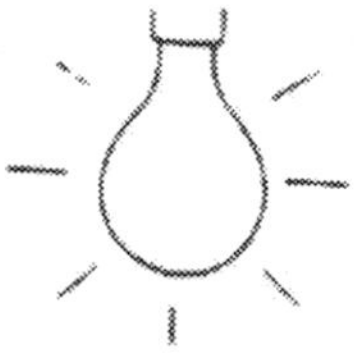   JET

4 VOLCANIC    PIN

5 DIM 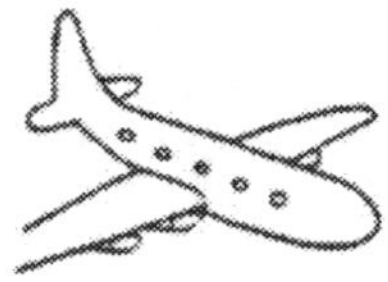   CAN

6 LIMP    ROCK

---

1 SAD   LEG

2 SPLIT     FACT

3 SILK    MOP

4 RAG    TANK

5 LEFT 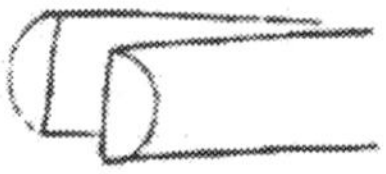   LOG

JACK'S STILL SICK.

6 FULL 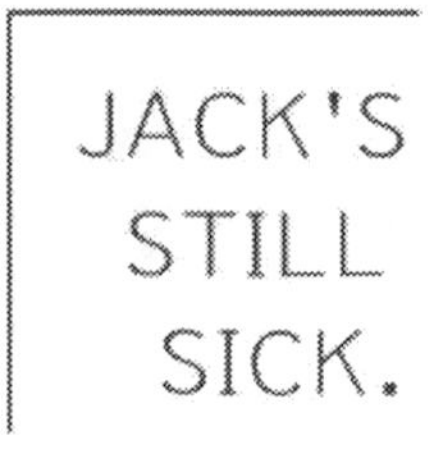   FLAG

1 AN ANT'S NOT BIG

2 BUT IT CAN TWIST OFF AN INSECT'S LEG

3 AND DRAG IT UP AN ANT HILL.

1 HANK'S FAT PIG SAT IN ITS PEN.

2 HANK FED IT SLOP AND SCRAPS.

3 IT GRUNTED AND ACTED GLAD.

1 RICK'S DOG SPOT FELL

2 AND TWISTED ITS LEG.

3 RICK HELD SPOT STILL

1 TILL DOC HANCOCK GOT SPLINTS ON IT.

2 IT WILL SWELL

3 AND GET STIFF

1 BUT WILL NOT GET INFECTED.

2 HOT PACKS AND REST

3 WILL HELP SPOT GET BETTER QUICK.

1 DOT'S GOT PAT'S BIG WIG ON AND

2 CAN'T TELL IT'S DAMP AND SLICK.

3 DOT SLIPS AND TRIPS.

1 MOM HELPS DOT STAND UP.

2 DOT GOT PAT'S WIG WET.

3 MOM WILL FLUFF IT UP.

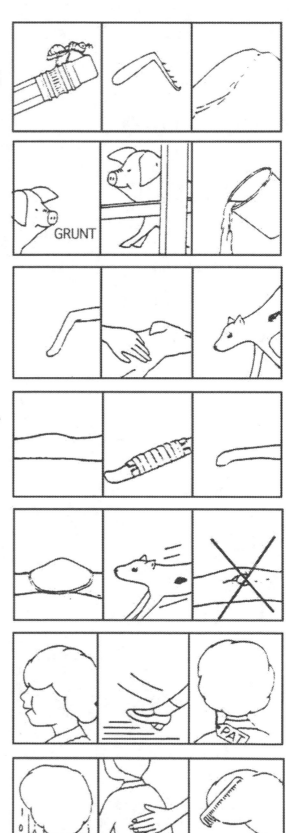

1 GRILL  HAM

2 JACK UP  PLANTS

3 PULL OFF  TRUCKS

4 UNPLUG MILK AND NUTMEG

5 DIG UP  MASKS

6 MIX LAMPS

---

1 RENT BUMPS

2 RUB 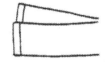 SNACKS

3 GULP EXITS

4 BLOCK SLACKS

5 PRINT LAND

6 HEM  LISTS

1 QUINT'S LAMP HAD AN ODD BULB.

2 IT WENT WINK, WINK, OFF AND ON.

3 QUINT HAD JUST GOT IN BED

1 AND OFF IT WENT.

2 QUINT SQUINTED AT IT

3 BUT DID NOT TWIST IT.

1 QUINT LET DAD FIX IT.

2 AT LAST IT WENT BACK ON.

3 IT LIT UP QUINT'S RED AND BLACK QUILT.

1 QUINT LIFTED IT UP,

2 GOT UNDER IT,

3 AND SLEPT.

1 GLEN: WILL STAN SELL US MINTS AND
            GUM?

2 PEG: MINTS AND GUM AND POP.

3 GLEN: WILL MINTS COST LESS?

1 PEG: YES, GLEN, MINTS WILL COST

2 GLEN: LET'S GET MINTS.

3 PEG: NOT MINTS! GUM!

1 GLEN: NOT JUST GUM! GUM AND
            PEPPERMINTS.

2 PEG: STAN, SELL US SIX PEPPERMINTS.

3 GLEN: AND PEPPERMINT GUM. TEN
            STICKS.

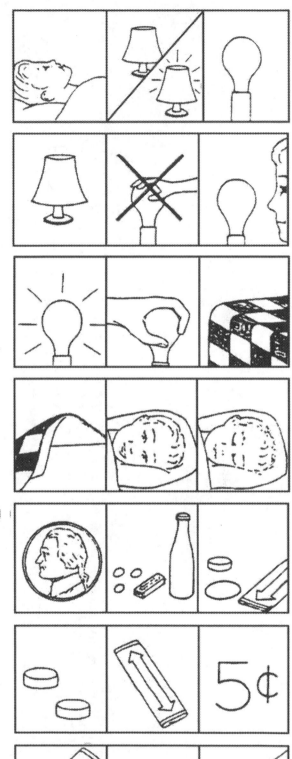

49

ax		JUG
bug		DOG
cat		LEG
dog		FULL
egg		AX
full		INK
gum		HAT
hat		CAT
ink		MOP
jug		BUG
kick		EGG
leg		GUM
mop		KICK

nut

ox

pot

quill

rat

sip

tack

up

vest

wet

x (eks)

yak

zip

X

POT

TACK

NUT

WET

UP

SIP

QUILL

YAK

VEST

OX

ZIP

RAT

```
P  I  K  R  A  R  O  X  P  D  W  S  D  B  C  A  C
Z  G  Q  F  U  B  G  V  G  I  U  X  P  O  G  U  A
R  N  S  P  W  Z  B  R  T  L  B  C  A  C  I  T  H
F  Q  L  G  P  M  Y  I  O  V  C  N  K  S  Y  O  T
A  R  O  D  U  H  Y  X  T  J  H  W  P  O  F  A  W
Q  F  U  O  E  R  A  N  F  D  R  C  B  T  U  K  B
I  Z  J  I  N  Y  I  S  T  C  M  A  D  A  B  O  Q
N  F  T  O  Q  J  X  F  K  X  S  R  T  S  N  W
S  E  C  Y  U  X  C  M  O  E  X  G  K  B  V  S  K
H  M  J  B  Q  G  E  H  E  Y  G  L  S  Q  N  C
S  K  G  W  L  E  F  T  P  A  P  E  H  O  U  R  D
L  Q  U  N  I  P  K  O  Y  U  Z  R  L  H  Y  B  U
H  J  Z  T  K  G  I  P  K  D  W  L  I  D  E  P  M
V  R  A  V  I  E  O  M  P  O  X  K  M  T  V  L  S
G  N  L  S  U  H  R  Y  T  E  W  N  F  S  T  X  N
U  J  Y  A  S  O  N  F  S  Q  R  U  X  B  I  E  Z
```

UPP ————   OGD ————   GROF _____   NITTEK _____

GIP ————   GUB ————   NEH _____   KAY _____

TAN ————   TAC ————   TIBBAR _____   TINSEC _____

OFX ————   KUNSK _____   DUISQ _____   SABS _____

XO ————   TAR _____   KUCD _____   HASSGROPPER _____

Answers p. 55 Have learners practice writing small letters in solving the puzzle.

Horizontal _____

Vertical |

53

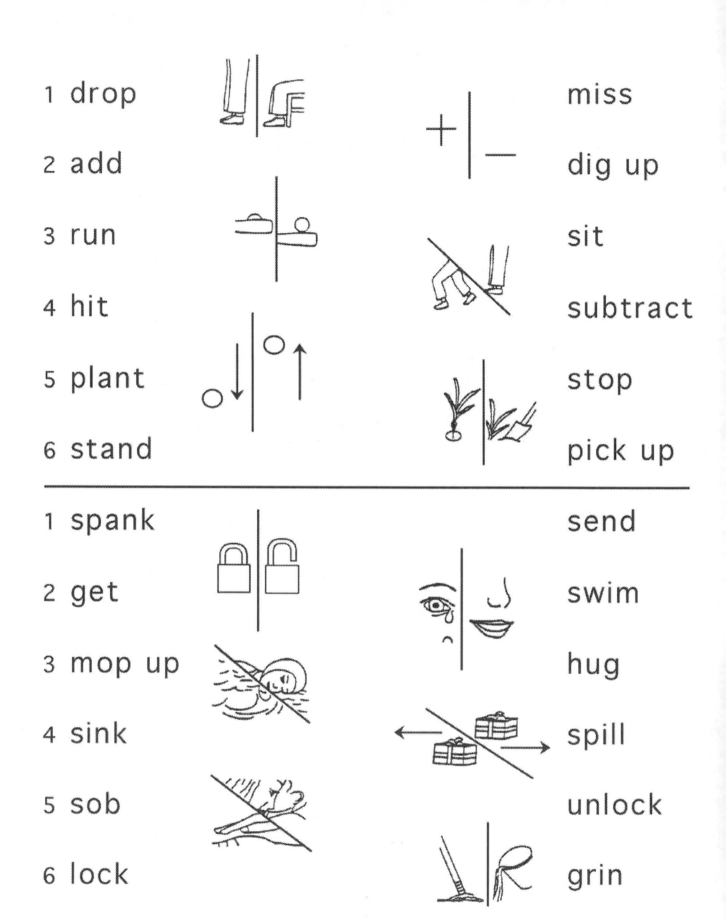

1 drop   miss

2 add   dig up

3 run   sit

4 hit   subtract

5 plant   stop

6 stand   pick up

1 spank   send

2 get   swim

3 mop up   hug

4 sink   spill

5 sob   unlock

6 lock   grin

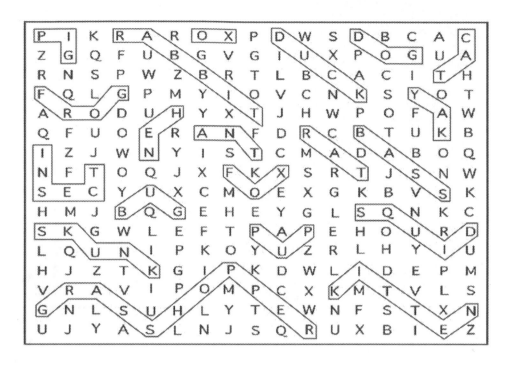

UPP	PUP	OGD	DOG	GROF	FROG	NITTEK	KITTEN
GIP	PIG	GUB	BUG	NEH	HEN	KAY	YAK
TAN	ANT	TAC	CAT	TIBARB	RABBIT	TINSEC	INSECT
OFX	FOX	KUNSK	SKUNK	DUISQ	SQUID	SABS	BASS
XO	OX	TAR	RAT	KUCD	DUCK	HASSGROPPER	GRASSHOPPER

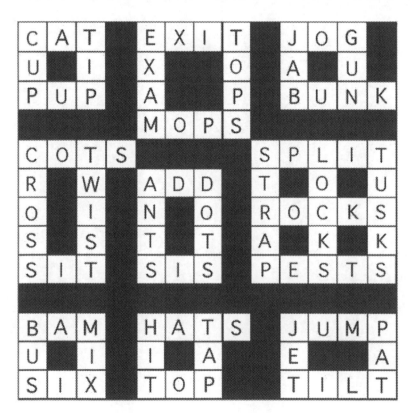

✦Our first step.
✦Our first word.
✦Reading and writing our first words.
✦Four of life's most shining moments.

Sadly, we are actually falling behind countries like Bolivia and Cuba in terms of literacy, where a nearly perfect Spanish alphabet and spelling makes learning so rapid and easy. **The Training Wheels Alphabet Book** actually surpasses Spanish in terms of regularity, allowing leaners to shine as brightly as anyone anywhere from the very first moment.

To simplify and accelerate learning to read and write, **The Training Wheels Alphabet Book** employs regularly spelled words only. Each letter always represents the same phoneme. Letter-sound correspondences are firmly fixed in learners' minds through novel exercises based on numerous non-complex illustrations on every page.

Our traditional English spelling is so irregular that its 41 phonemes can be represented in 561 ways. To get learners off to a fast, confidence-building start, **The Training Wheels Alphabet Book** employs exclusively regular spellings, reducing this to a mere 26.

Each grapheme invariably represents the same phoneme, the one with which it is most commonly associated. For example, A always stands for its sound in *at*, not *ate*, *above*, or *always*. E as in *met*, not *meet*, *great*, *sieve*, or *shovel*. I as in *lit*, not *light*, *rabbit* or *kilo*. O as in *tot*, not *tote*, *took* or love. U as in *cut*, not *cute*, *dude*, *dour* or *four*. S as in *hiss*, never *his*, *sugar*, *fish* or *vision*. C as in *cat*, not *cease* or *delicious*. G as in *go*, not *gym*….Etc.

Each grapheme, together with its accompanying phoneme, is systematically introduced and then reviewed in a variety of ways. Learning is active, not passive. Children (and others who so desire) may color the varied letter-sound depictions as an added way to keep them permanently in mind.

Irregular letter-sound correspondences are introduced in **The *Look, Mom, No Hands* Alphabet Book, Poor Little Sick Boy**, and additional **Easy Speedy Readers®**.